SECRETS

KHADJ ROUF

The Children's Society · London

First published in 1989
by The Children's Society
Edward Rudolf House, Margery Street,
London WC1X 0JL

British Library Cataloguing in Publication Data

Rouf, Khadj, *1968–*
Secrets.
1. Children. Sexual abuse by adults
I. Title II. Church of England,
Children's Society
362.7′044

ISBN 0–907324–37–1

Typeset by Goodfellow & Egan
Phototypesetting Ltd, Cambridge.
Printed by Purnell Book Production Ltd, Bristol.

Introduction

I was asked to write an introduction to this book but now I'm sitting here I'm not really sure what I'm supposed to say.

My message is in the words and pictures of my story – a story that I lived through for many years of my childhood.

I have written this story for children and teenagers who may be going through the same thing. I have written it because I was tired of all the books designed to warn us against *strangers* when often it is someone we *know* who decides to abuse us.

I feel so angry that even though we're told that we're not to blame for what has happened we are never allowed to say who we really are.

The past is part of everyone: why should I have to deny my past? How could I ever go forward if I was never allowed to look back?

I was a victim. Knowing that has helped me to fight. Now I'm a survivor.

That's why my name is on the front of these books. I'm not afraid any more. The only one who should be afraid knows his name.

So I leave you with my words and my pictures and I hope they will help every victim to find the courage that he or she has inside him or herself.

The courage to tell and to survive.

Khadj
1988

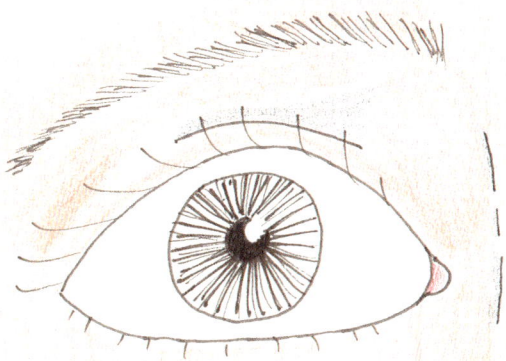

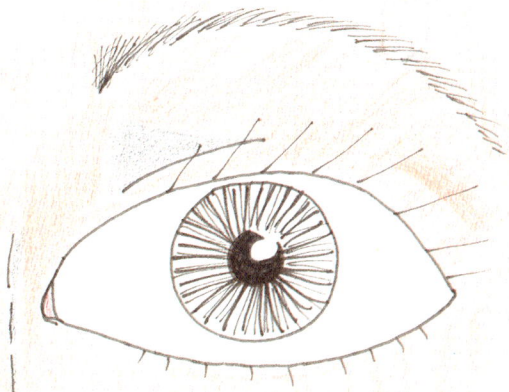

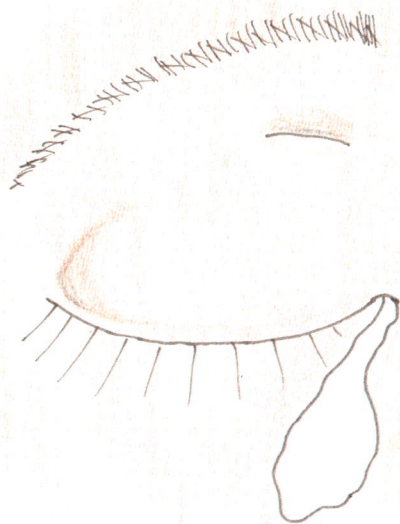

REMEMBER CHILDREN! IF YOUR DAD, OR ANYONE ELSE IN YOUR FAMILY DOES THOSE THINGS AND SAYS THOSE THINGS SO THAT YOU FEEL BAD, TELL SOMEONE!
- AND IF YOU THINK THAT YOUR MUM WON'T BELIEVE YOU TELL SOMEONE ELSE
...BECAUSE YOUR DAD MAY START TO DO THINGS TO YOUR BROTHERS AND SISTERS TOO.
PLEASE TELL — SOMEONE IS BOUND TO BELIEVE YOU.